Exchanging Wisdom

A Guide for Parents of the Autonomous

Exchanging Wisdom
A Guide for Parents of the Autonomous

Christopher Luna

with

Angelo Luna

A Publication of The Poetry Box

Editing & Book Design by Shawn Aveningo Sanders
Cover Design by Shawn Aveningo Sanders

ISBN: 978-1-948461-96-2
Library of Congress Control Number: 2021939952
Printed in the United States of America.
Wholesale Distribution via Ingram.

Published by The Poetry Box ®, December 2021
    under The Poetry Box Select imprint
Portland, Oregon
ThePoetryBox.com

Poems for Angelo

Contents

All poems by Christopher Luna except where noted.

Afterword

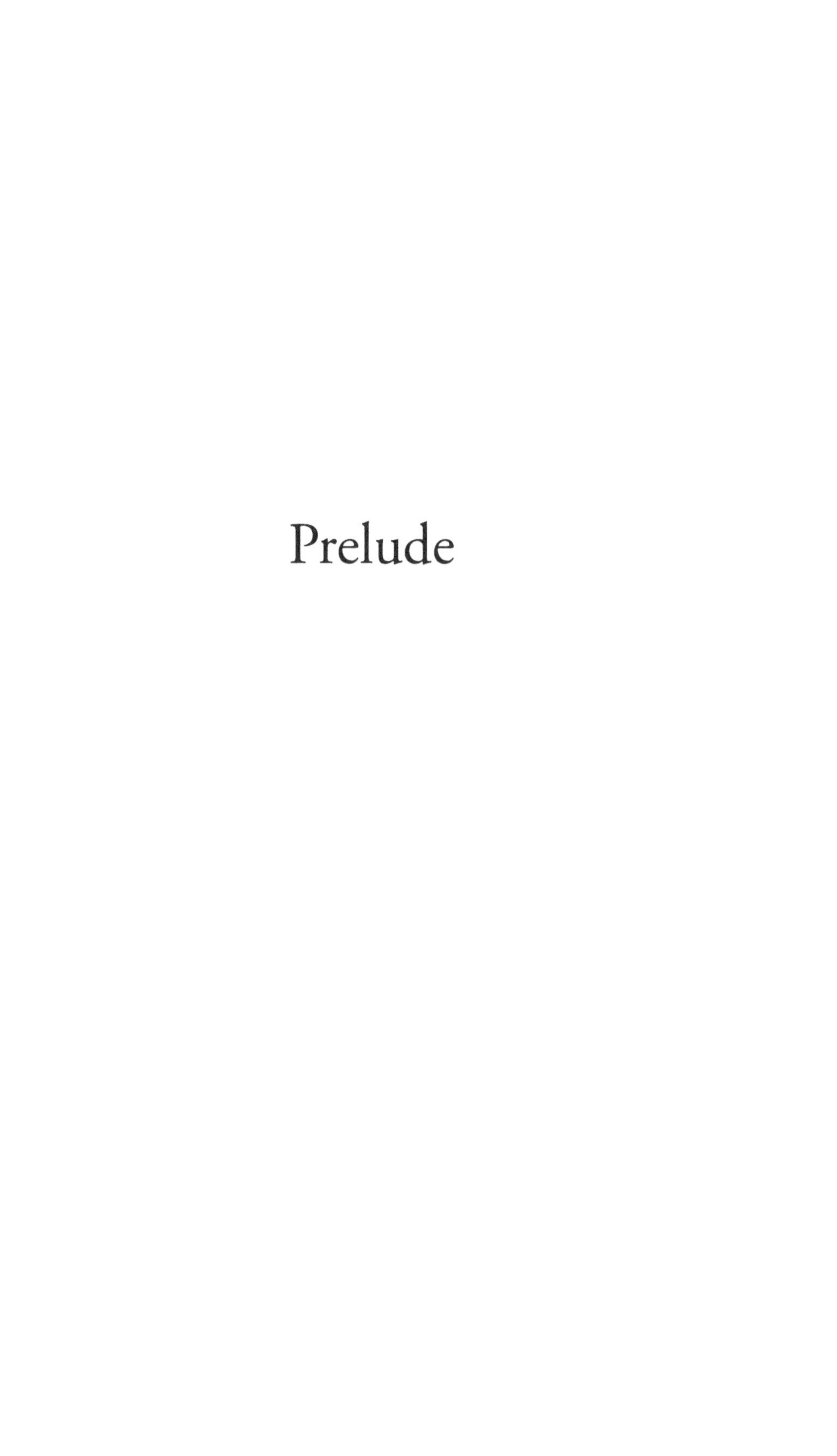

Prelude

Angelo's First Poem

Composed in the Car, August 2002

Old

yellow

fan

had a

pipe.

Note: Angelo's mother and I lived together as I studied for my graduate degree at the Jack Kerouac School of Disembodied Poetics. From the moment that she moved to Boulder to live with me, our plan was to return to New York (where we had met) after school was over. Living with my parents in Levittown, Long Island while Dahnn was pregnant was neither ideal nor easy, but I soon found a job with the H. W. Wilson Company in the Bronx, a more than one-hundred-year-old publisher that had once employed Stanley Kunitz. We found a place in Richmond Hill, Queens, in the same neighborhood where my parents had lived when I was born. I commuted using the D, F, and J trains, and read long books like *Ulysses* on the subway, writing down overheard conversation spoken by my fellow passengers. I have since told writers that in New York City, all one needs is to be conscious and have a pen and paper ready, and the poem presents itself to you. I was living the life I had always dreamed of: making a living as a writer in the city I love. I began as a staff writer and quickly advanced to being an editor. Soon Dahnn announced that she intended to return to Washington State, where she was born and raised. I say "announced" because there was no

[. . .]

conversation about her new plan. I was not consulted, nor were my feelings taken into account. In fact, I was informed that she would be moving home with my son whether I accompanied her or not. Knowing that I could not be Angelo's father from the other side of the country, I assented. The move was disastrous for me, both personally and professionally. I was out of work for the longest period of time since age 11, and I had no friends or contacts to help me establish myself. Angelo saved my ass. At the lowest point in my life, he was a constant source of joy. It felt wrong to be sad, wrong not to enjoy every second my underemployment allowed me to have with him. Eventually I met the love of my life and began nurturing literary community in Southwest Washington. Everything worked out, but it was all in spite of Angelo's mother. To read the rest of my answer to the oft-asked question "How the hell did you end up in Vancouver, WA?" check out my introduction to the first volume of the Ghost Town Poetry Open Mic anthologies I edited with Toni Lumbrazo Luna for Printed Matter Vancouver.

An Excerpt from "more than we can bear"

an investigative poem about the terrorist attacks
on September 11, 2001

He was thrown into a wall on the 55th floor of 1 World Trade Center when the first plane hit. He asked Jesus not to let the floor give way. He was a magical person. He loved Christmas and all things American. He was tough to argue with. He believed in being prepared. She believed in living for the moment. He was always thinking on his feet, and wanted you to think on your feet, too. He had started thinking about the yin and the yang of things. She had recently been promoted to operations manager. He loved to take care of the people around him. He was killed by falling debris. He died with very valuable things, valuable things in terms of his life.

July/August 2002

Dear Son,

I write this letter in anticipation of your future inquiries, which I suspect are moments away from bursting forth, as your secret and exponentially developing vocabulary is revealed to us. I don't know whether I can provide adequate answers – perhaps all I will be able to offer you are my observations, accompanied by countless questions of my own. But I will try, and I solemnly promise never to pretend to know that which I do not.

It was truly a beautiful morning, clear blue skies. And even before the buildings came crashing down the words began to fall like those who saw no choice but to jump to their deaths that day. Phone calls were made, and stories told, and re-told, as the world

[. . .]

we'd known changed before our eyes. New York became the USA, and the USA became New York. And we learned to breathe and smile and laugh and appreciate beauty again but never completely erased it from our minds. Questions needed to be asked. Shifts forced initiated endured. Lines blurred drawn penetrated. The desire to retreat into denial was strong. Even body counts were subject to debate. Games that served to distract. From the Fact? That mutually assured destruction was back in fashion, and in fact, had never gone out of style at all. Out of work. We did not flee the city. Merely chose the wrong time to relocate. 10 months. Some anniversaries do not inspire celebration. I learned that we all want to love and be loved in return, and that we all want to be free, and that we all want to go home. Phrases carry weight linger dissipate. Language struggles again to describe what is ineffable. The fact that this may be impossible need not prevent our attempts from yielding objects of great beauty. That day. September 11, the moment we couldn't get out of, yielded far more death and destruction than occurred in the attacks that day. And with every bomb dropped, every shot fired, every arrogant threatening statement made by our so-called leaders, we gave birth to future terrorists. As I write, the fascists have taken control, and plot to destroy the world. Our precious freedoms will not survive if the bloodthirsty theocrats are allowed to have their way.

> fatherhood inspires
> a newfound appreciation
> for the inevitability of death

> peril everywhere &
>   soon he will be big enough
>   to step out into it

>   no
>   don't do that
>   don't eat the Buddha
>   that's not to eat
>   not edible

Do all children resemble sleeping angels, or are their parents the only ones predisposed to recognize the angel in them? I don't know, but I am certain that you were aptly named, Angelo. I knew the moment you slipped forth into our world.

> must he learn of the suffering
> the ubiquity of the unkind?
>
> does he have to know
> frustration, loss, disappointment
> can't I shield him from it somehow please?

The most difficult question you've asked so far is "Are you sad?" I don't want you to be sheltered from the realities of this world, but nor do I want to violate the protection your innocence provides before you are ready.

> how to explain rape murder lynching genocide?
> how do I tell him that sometimes puppies don't make it?
> > that great thinkers are silenced?
> > that President Clinton left Peltier to die in jail?

I have rejected organized religion because it has been and continues to be the primary catalyst for hatred, ignorance, and barbarism. I don't trust anyone who claims to possess the ability to know that which cannot be known. And I don't trust anyone who believes that their life – or the lives of others who think, speak, live, and pray as they do – is more valuable than that of another.

So I oppose war, although I have wondered whether it isn't a force of nature, as some have suggested. But I have decided to speak out nevertheless. Change only comes when people are moved to act, when they make some noise.

[. . .]

I suppose that when it's time for you to assert your individuality and rebel against my authority, you'll most likely become a Republican, or conveniently find Jesus. But your father is no fool. Neither of the two extremely limited major political parties in this country have a monopoly on hate, stupidity, greed. And until they are beholden to their constituents rather than rich folk and corporations, I reject both of them on principle.

> I can no longer tolerate news stories about dead babies,
> mangled babies, murdered babies, drowned babies,
> strangled and abused babies, neglected and burned babies
> I have no stomach for it.

I suppose what I have learned over the course of three decades is that the act of questioning is far more significant than any answers we might receive. So hold on to that inquisitiveness some mistakenly claim is unique to children. Open your heart, and be on the lookout for people, or beliefs, that threaten to leave you in "chains of mind locked up."

> quiet rare   this thought
> this time   this tone
> this crime   no crime
>   only sweet sustenance
>   my boy's smile
>   as he greets me at the door

Life can be joy, and heartbreak, and suffering, and wonder, and understanding. It can be a lot of things, but if you pay close attention, it is seldom boring. Get ready for an incredible adventure. Beauty surrounds us. Live in the present. Have fun.

There are many things that I do not know, and many things that I cannot explain. Your Daddy is not a superhero; he's just a guy who loves you with all his heart, and a man determined to keep you out of harm's way, to ensure that you always fall to sleep knowing that you are loved.

Go ahead kid – wave at the shadow.

Love,
Dad

He worked as a vice president of risk services at Marsh & McLennan, on the 100th floor of tower one. She worked hard as an assistant bond trader for Cantor Fitzgerald, and she was a veteran of the 1993 World Trade Center bombing. He first played CBGB when he was seventeen, with a band called the Psychotics. He stayed true to himself. He really had his life in order. He was always in motion. He always had to be moving. He got along well with everybody and was being groomed to be a long-timer. He just couldn't stop crying. He said, "Mommy, something hit the building, and I need to tell you I love you. I love all of you.

Note: the descriptions of the victims above were extracted from the *New York Times* series "Portraits of Grief" as well as similar remembrances found in *Newsday.*

Exchanging Wisdom

from "Snapshots of Kelso"

my son is a joy and a wonder
with a laugh all his own
and more faces than Lon Chaney
and he is sweet and charming
and mischievous and infuriating

every moment he offers me
another opportunity to fuck up
and sometimes I do

on our way to the train station
Angelo hands me a tiny leaf
objects to my unimaginative terminology:

 "That's not a leaf, it's a heart."

 "It's a heart? Well, then, I'll keep it and treasure it always."

Angelo Discovers Dizzy

August 2003

Let's look

at the book

    with the picture of

Dizzy's cheeks.

Let's look at Dizzy's cheeks.
It was fun lookin' at Dizzy's cheeks.

    This is Is, and you're listening to Astrology

    This is Machito.
    Where is the car?
    Where is your piano?

    Is this Machito? It sounds like him.
    I think she gonna play some Dizzy.

    Speaking of Diz, we're gonna send out a request to Angelo,
    he's a three-year-old Dizzy Gillespie fan who called in.
    So this one goes out to Angelo.

        Oo-bla-bi-da
        hi-ho my bee ho
        Short, paunchy naunch nose.
        Don't dance so hard. Don't boogie.
        Hoogie boogie baunch nose.
        Hoogie boogie traunch nose.

    Dizzy Gillespie? The person who blows real hard?
    The waterfall on my meat. The basket still swinging.

Paddywack on the snow.
Knicknack on his body.
Unch unch unch unch UNCH!
Unchie unchie unchie unchie.

> I'm playing horns thorns but Dizzy letter 8-9.

Dizzy played trumpet. Dizzy played the saxophone.
Dizzy. Does it make your cheeks *so* big?
> Does it make your cheeks so big?

Astrology was a program on Portland's KBOO Radio (90.7 FM)

The Last Fight

Daddy went to sleep with coffee grounds in his hair,
and the sincere hope that this will be the final argument.

Nothing left to say.
Nothing left to do but escalate.

Seeing your tiny hands pressed over your ears
as you sleep is all the convincing I'll ever need.

I'll be picking shards of glass out of the carpet for weeks.

Our strife is so routine that not even the death of my godfather
will interrupt it. Long for New York, for the life I was forced
to leave behind, but I cannot be without you.

Men leave because they can.
But don't you worry.
Daddy isn't going anywhere.

Angelo Picks Flowers for Dad and Ganesh

The power of the book only lasts for a little time.
This is one of my gifts for you. Soon this will end.
     It is only temporary. Look, you found it.
          The Rock of Liberty!

I'm helping you get as much of that stuff as I can.
'Cause it's one of my gifts. Remember to tell me
if you see any more of those dandelions, Dad. I'll BLOW 'EM!
In my world, everything is perfect.
You can't be in it. Everyone has their own world.
No grownups at my ceremony. They don't allow grownups
at my church. I can bring you back a piece of cake from my ceremony.

       Wanna do some research? I want you to go on my world
         if you're doing research right now.

That's another one of the gifts I give to you.
I try to give you all the leaves that I can.
Did you know that Ganesh's gifts are your gifts
     that I'm trying to give you?
I want you to play gambling so you can win money.

     You have to find your real bride.
     Your real bride is a rock star with a blue guitar.

     I like giving you gifts.
     These are the source of the power good.
     Give my word deep and rise.
     This shall tell us the way back home.

Every word in this poem was uttered by my son Angelo in April or July of 2006.

A Warning

January 26, 2007

1.

I'm writing it all down for you:
    collecting and cataloguing
    the many moments
    which have made up
        my life

the life I had before
the miracle of your birth
and the life I've shared with you
        since being forced
        to leave home

            you have become
            my collaborator
            and my greatest teacher
            and all of my time with you

(including each moment I have longed to be back in New York)

                has been a precious gift
                I wouldn't trade
                    for anything

        but if I don't make it
        you may have to
        embark upon a mission
            to recover
            one or two
            lost works

there are always
several sides
to every story
each with its own
    legitimacy

I'm trying to get it all down

later, after I'm gone
it would be a mistake
    to assume
that you have the whole picture

2.

For a brief moment I was free

    making a living as a writer
    and we were living
    in Richmond Hill

    not too far from Kerouac's Ozone Park

    around the corner from the apartment
    my parents had taken my newborn self to

I was a subway recontextualist
    hopped up on minutiae
I was this guy running around New York City
    ripped out of my mind
    with excitement

[. . .]

But when it came time to stand up
        I stood down
abandoning a city
still recovering from the loss of nearly 3,000
        on September 11

        they did not check our truck on the way out of The City

in fact, sent us packing
without license plates
and all the way from Jersey
        to Columbus
        to Kansas City
        to Boulder
        to Washington
we were not pulled over once

For a brief moment   I was free

                             Now I'm doing time
                             sentenced to sixteen years
                             locked down in Ghost Town
                             choking on the bitter taste
                             of dreams deferred   years lost
                             choking on the backwater

Things Get Serious in Ghost Town

walking home from Clark College
Dick Cheney passed me
driving a blood red pickup
don't have to remind you
about the gas mileage
on a vehicle like that

the deep-seated belief
that the suburbs are somehow insulated
from the violence and insanity of The City
is a Myth created by frightened white folks
who whisper to one another like children
playing beneath forts made of bedsheets

                                  casting spells
                                  to ward off Evil

for even here in Vancouver, USA
things have been getting serious
kidnapping, murder, shooting, stabbing
much of it, if you believe the papers,
        committed by skeletal raccoons
        tweaked out on methamphetamine

last night while I was in bed
the boy's arms wrapped tightly around my neck
            a woman ran through my neighborhood screaming
              and it was for his sake, I told myself
        that I did not run outside to aid her
          but instead lay there, frozen
            and listened

The Life of John Thomas

January 12, 2008

Angelo's classmate
little John Thomas
destined to take the 'Couve by storm
plays in the bushes
with the girls after school
and wonders about
        the smile
at the corner of teacher's mouth
each time she calls his name.

At Angelo's Bedside

Nothing in this world
makes a parent feel more helpless
than a boy's anguished cries –
nurses nowhere to be found.

Good thing
there is more than one way
for a father to "provide"
or I'd be the asshole
in this painting.

Spencer Puts the Whammy
on Angelo's Innards

Angelo informs me
that his appendix
became inflamed
     after Spencer
     the class bully
cursed him with The Evil Eye:

"There was smoke comin' out of his eye, Dad."

A Philosophical Discourse
on the Nature of Good and Evil
while Walking Home from School

April 23, 2008

Angelo remains disturbed
having witnessed his friend Jonathan's face
hit the floor in Dance class
cutting open his chin
to expose "the meat."

In a quick reverse of his previous declaration
that God does not exist
he informs me that God and The Devil
are inside each of us
and control what we do.

Angelo lets me know that he frequently
chooses Transylvania over Happysville
which allows The Devil to influence him
to do Evil things
such as conspire with Azure
to set a muddy trap for his grandmother
or wrestle his cousin Elan
        into submission.

I remind him of his utter sweetness
yet he remains convinced
that his heart belongs to The Devil
and he is destined to do wrong.

Death Becomes Real

On Thursday evening, May 1, 2008, Angelo came face-to-face with the inevitability of Death. Although we had discussed Death before, it was on this occasion that I witnessed an event that is a rite of passage for all children: I watched his face change as the reality of his father's eventual demise became horribly, inescapably real.

> "I wish you could get more rest. When we get home, you want me to massage your shoulders? Staying alive is much more important than catching a bus. Did you know I'm still gonna be alive in 2045? Will you? I hope so. I wish you would never die….Can I have some snuggles?"

Before I was diagnosed with and treated for sleep apnea, I tended to lose energy around three o'clock, which just happened to be the time of day when Angelo had the most energy for playing with his father.

Watching *Inland Empire* with an Eight-Year-Old Is Not Responsible Parenting

August 2, 2008

Even before I invited my son to sit down with us
I was aware that Mr. Lynch's films
approximate the experience of another person's nightmare
so I should not have been surprised at Angelo's terror
when The Phantom's maniacal, distorted face appeared

I may have mistaken his bravery for immunity.
Who knows how often his rest has been disturbed
by visits from Two-Face or second-rate prime-time zombies?

Who knows what effect the burned chunks of
the mutilated soldier in *In the Valley of Elah*
      had on his young mind?

Who can blame him for worrying
that some harm will come to me in the night?
For holding me tight and whispering "be safe"
each time his mother picks him up from my place?

The Buddha of Independence Day

September 2008

Angelo leads me through the desert. I follow behind him, reading from a hardcover book full of his future poems. As we explore the wasteland, he informs me about the gods, their powers, and their stations:

> "You know the Buddha, right? The one who comes on the Fourth of July. I know a lot about the gods. Ganesh is the fifth god. The first one is the Emperor of Heaven, the one we don't believe in. It's true. If you don't believe it's true it means you don't believe in Ganesh's powers. Sin is one of the 15 devils. He's enemies with Ganesh, but of course, Ganesh always wins. Did you know that Cat is the god of China? Remember that trick I invented? I named it the Flying Me. I'm the Great Corrector. I am your alternative. Jedi Raccoon. I paused the Seven Trials. I think this year the chaos orbs are aligning."

from *Ghost Town, USA*

November 6, 2008

It's Sunday night. I answer a knock on the door. It's Craig, offering an invitation to a Bible class at Fort Vancouver High School. "It's not my thing," I reply, "but thanks anyway." After I shut the door, Angelo reminds me that I am wearing a t-shirt that reads: "RECOVERING CHRISTIAN."

from "Ode to Cathleen Luna, the O.G. (Original Goddess)"

Mother's Day 2009

When I was a teen, if you saw me scribbling in one of my notebooks, you'd jokingly ask if I was writing about how wonderful my mother is. I confess that this was not always the case. However, I wrote with the awareness that none of the adventures I was having would have been possible without you.

I occasionally ask Angelo to promise me that he will remain sweet forever. "There isn't enough sweetness in the world," I tell him. "So you'll be doing a good thing if you hold on to that." When he throws his arms around me, tells me "I love you, you're the best Dad in the world," or brings me flowers, I am filled with an indescribable joy, and the knowledge that he is a living embodiment of the love *you* created. A love which will outlive us all.

Lost Arts

May 18, 2009

Angelo and Jake are still young enough
to pull back the veil
to reveal holes torn
in the space-time continuum

                vanishing fences
                unexplained electromagnetic occurrences
                ghostly shotgun blasts

when Angelo grows up
he intends to become
        a scientist
in order to prove
that there is an alternate reality

a place where
the conclusions to our dreams
happen the next day

            follow us out
            of the recesses
            of the mind

                    into the hallway
                    into the light

Making Our Escape from 919 U St., Apt. K

screens loose
concrete steps crumbling
tires under stairs
this New Yorker sleeps with a baseball bat close by
silent ghostly Eastern European
       in shades stalks parking lot
       talking on his cell phone
       suspiciously carries handtruck
       and shovel up and down the stairs
mouse inside oven
squirrel behind dishwasher
frog under baby bella mushrooms
       in the fridge
serial killer in the apt. below
smokes, yells at the Hawaiian kids next door
called landlord to complain about
toddlers running around upstairs
mellows considerably after his
Asian mail order brides arrive
used to scowl, walk on by
now smiles and greets me with a "Howdy"
amazing what a proper lay can do for a man
even in this tenement of horrors

Three Crows on a Wire

In Angelo's nightmares, his father appears in triplicate
and it is his challenge to defeat the impostors
to determine which of the three is for real.

He tells me about this dilemma on the walk home from school
and asks for advice on how
to apply lucid dreaming toward a solution.

All three of you are he—
he must make the correct choice
or risk killing me.

The power of words diminishes
before the abyss
of the subconscious.

A place I cannot go—
even as my son screams out
to be rescued.

[if only I could hear]

if only I could hear
the song in his head
as he plans his moves
avoids a kick to the balls
faces a black belt
or, more frequently
is shuttled
from father
to uncle
to mother
to grandmother
and back

Prophecy

beginning with a line by Angelo (Age 9)

As far as you're concerned, I came from the sky.
I am the beam which cleaves that cloud.
That notion you'd left behind.
I set my hand upon you, and you are restored.
You have agency.
Breathe deep and step forward.
Liberation is available to those who give themselves permission.
Those who can envision. Be vulnerable.
Put theory into practice. Accept responsibility.

from *Ghost Town, USA*

December 21, 2009 – June 12, 2010

December 21, 2009

After Mr. Yu presents Angelo
with his first belt
for tae kwon do   (white with blue stripe)
he tells me that he has enjoyed working with my son
watching him come out of his shell

Mr. Yu tells me that Angelo has a sharp mind
and that this is far more important to the martial artist
because while muscles can be developed
a strong intellect is much harder to obtain

On our way to Dahnn's place
listening to Z100
(hoping it's a phase the boy's going through)
I am overcome by Jay-Z and Alicia Keys
weeping silently to myself upon hearing
"Empire State of Mind"
dreaming of home
               contemplating
               sacrifice

#32 Eastbound
April 8, 2010

On the way home from school
Angelo and I discuss *Alice in Wonderland*
the new videogame he bought with his birthday money
because he knows that his Dad likes the story

suddenly the young man sitting across from us
holds out a white plastic spoon
and informs us that this is the spoon
he used to invent all videogames

        though Angelo understands
        that the stranger is delusional
        he plays along:
                        "Like God of War and Lego Star Wars?"

        Angelo holds the spoon
        for a few moments
        then gives it back

                "I guess you'll be needing that," I comment

soon the young man
begins behaving erratically
reaches into his bag
a rifle manual falls onto
the bus floor

I try to get us off the bus quickly
explaining to Angelo
that delusional people can sometimes
hurt themselves or others
but that this is no reason to humiliate them
        or mock them

I tell him how proud I am
of how he handled it

        he gets it

then I explain that some of us
believe that there is some truth hidden
in the ravings of madmen

> as we turn the corner
> we hear a sound
> that resembles a jackhammer

> and laugh together
> as we notice

> a woodpecker
> perched on a streetlight

> tapping away
> apparently lacking the natural instinct
> to tell the difference between metal and wood

June 12, 2010

I used to draw every day
lose myself in endless fields of light
fall into reams of blank
fill them up with longhaired,
muscle-bound heroes
beasts, aliens, wizards
of my imagination.

At some point the images retreated
from my hand into my head
where I allowed them more time to spin
before releasing them.

Decades later
I am moved to put Sharpie to paper
        once again
attempting to capture
the essence of
a hand, a foot,
a pair of lips.

I bring a sketchbook to my son's taekwondo class.

Capturing the most familiar parts of the body is *not* easy,
        not like a riding a bike.

It is *fucking hard*
to draw his nose
without causing it to balloon
in one direction
or another.

The drawings are not perfect.
I want so badly for them to be perfect.
Don't we all? Yet on the one day
that I refrain from sketching,
the boy is disappointed.
I try again.

The Ballad of Banshee Bob

May 19, 2011

To hear the old folks in Ghost Town tell it
Banshee Bob had a singular ability to
shriek, barbecue, pwn newbs
catch Pikachu, honor Ganesh
imitate Michael Jackson
run, skip, sing
use his natural sweetness to charm the ladies
solve complex mathematical equations
employ his axe-kick
to dispatch with
overeager premilleniallists
end times fetishists
then laugh in the face of the faithful
on May 22, the day after the apocalypse
has failed to materialize
call the whole thing off
utilize kinesics to build a more peaceful community
prevent the zombie apocalypse
with a devastating elbow smash
make it home in time to
watch Chuck and Fringe with his Dad
and release a thousand unicorns from his butt

simultaneously
without breaking
the remotest hint
of a sweat

Don't believe me?
Just ask the ladies—they know what I'm talkin' about.

Father and Son, Facing the Same Way

thought rushes through
synapse vessel
like hypertensive blood
branching off in 60 directions at once

no way to stop the frenzy of the explosion
no way to escape the pileup
at the end of thought's path

still, it might be possible
to slow down enough
to see each
to experience each
one at a time

Words of Advice for Young People:
Father to Son Edition

Be kind.
Stay sweet:
for there is much rancor
in the world
and not enough sweetness.

> Be observer.
> Be participant.
> Shut up.
> Speak.
> Defend
> the defenseless.
> Look.
> Listen.
> Act.
> Think.

Judge not, judge all.

> The self-righteous are not beyond repair; we
> must help them realize that it is alright for
> others to be correct, on occasion. Opinions are
> like assholes. Mine no more important than
> yours, except when it is.

> Never stop learning.
> Distrust your laurels.
> Read your press, but don't believe it.
> You can always do better.
> Never allow the search to cease.
> There is always more to know.

Learn to notice how and when others flinch,
or wince, at the sound of your voice.

Try to love everyone, especially those you find impossible to like.
            But be careful not to oppress anyone with it—
                unwanted love is fascist, very uncool.

            Love yourself.
            Be good to yourself,
            then, keep it to yourself,
            unless you're at the microphone.

Christopher's Sketch of Angelo Luna Reading Poetry
at Paper Tiger Coffee, December 17, 2014

Wisp of a Rural Childhood Recollection

-for Doug Smith and Angelo Luna

sometimes the latticework of the veil
emerges before the eyes like floating tendrils swimming
curling in upon itself like a vortex
portal self-created
additional openings
sigh like hungry pores
myoclonic revelation
made suddenly external
long-hidden memory struggles to manifest
insight on the tip of your recall
like a recurring bronze sheet
borne anew from escaped synapse eel convulsion
skipping toward awaiting sunlight
the path makes itself known
will not remain still
will not behave
pops and twitches
demanding acknowledgment
fascinated with these rituals
collective unconscious
called forth
made flesh
mind's recesses rendered physically
maddeningly inaccessible
finally ineffable
ultimately unattainable

Wisdom Resides in a Young Man's Heart

little guy blows code
for the first time
applies mask
for the first time

becomes godhead
cannot prevent Truth
from flowing forth

not everyone accepts
the truth in
the secret
but all hear

none can deny
its rumbling majesty
its life-altering tremble
the orgasmic buzz
of its unassailable efficacy

the time has come
they are ready

Can you loan me your certitude?
May I borrow your fading blueprint?
Remove all questions from my mind?
Take your smile for a test drive?
Experience pure joy and wonder again?

law of attraction
a shaky proposition

comes down to faith
may have to recover
your sense of infinity
for a start

Questions for the Guru

The void is filled with the unfathomable sound of countless souls crying out in protest at the finite nature of their existence. When did hope steal away? How did we lose the ability to imagine infinity? How does one recover the key to the opening of the veil, the courage to step through the firmament and hurtle happily toward the dark matter? What lies beyond the mind's eye? What waits for us there? The answer must be out there somewhere. Couldn't possibly be right here, within me, could it? What are you afraid to find? What happened to your sense of adventure? Are these the right questions to ask?

Tiny Man Distracts from Contemplation of Infinity

how gently has night
secret lover
bound by neither vow
nor contract
delivered you into a circle of
ghostly deliverance
devoid of daylight's
mundanity?

every night
as I attempt
to fall to sleep
a tiny man
screams at me
from deep inside
the fibers of my pillow

admonishing me
ranting nonsense
and inscrutable mysticism
to distract me
from the contemplation
of infinity
to prevent me
from learning its
origins and meaning

mothers die
poets sicken

no stopping this deterioration

[. . .]

every chair at this table
will eventually empty

no substitution for the living, breathing lover

every brother
every sister
will expire

every sigh
every laugh
every cry
fade

what is left?
what remains?

how does one continue
after the duende has expired?

Fatherly Advice Dispensed in the Car
on the Way to School

beware the Jesus fish
an indirect threat
signaling bloodbath

vicious symbol
that warns:

    "Back off, Jack, or I will eat your family."

Aim Right for Their Third Eye

February 9, 2015

yes I know that it happens
I get that it's possible
but how often is one present
at the exact moment
that their offspring
first has their consciousness cracked open

        heart burst
        by truly grokking
        a great work of art?

after initially complaining about its lameness
Angelo stared into the Mona Lisa's left eye
until the tectonic plates shifted

     stars exploded

        and he was blasted through
        the doors of perception

and into the light
of a more interesting future

        a psychedelic freak show
        a cosmic love fest
        the Eternal Be-In

once you've opened those doors
you need never do so again....

Valerie's Family Photo Totally Destroys Me

Somewhere in the recesses of my memory resides the perpetual joy of watching your hair bounce as you ran from me, your little legs infused with boundless energy, your little head barely containing a consciousness bursting with limitless possibility. Like Lone Wolf and Cub we traversed the strange and passive-aggressive streets of Ghost Town, and I wrote down every word you said because they were brilliant. You reminded me that magic is real, that life is good, that despite your mother's concerted effort to destroy me, everything would eventually be OK. You saved my ass. You do not even realize that our adventures could have ended with the shadow of a horrible memory, a newspaper clipping reporting the violent end of a father who simply gave up. Thank you for every smile, every kiss, every time you challenged me or made me laugh. Your love makes every sacrifice worthwhile. You're not a little boy anymore, except in my heart's memory, and I can never thank you properly for bringing me back to life.

Sigil to Prevent the Spirit Death
of the Psychonaut

Catholic school sense memory
the constant Purgatory of fear

below and beyond the honeycomb tile
the solidity of the world recedes

I am safe
for as long as this
strange vision holds

later ego death
the twirling of the leaf
and the sudden separation of
the greens

                  doors of perception
                    remain open
                  for the duration

I cannot prove that
either of us is here
or that any of this is real
certain that I can't tell you
what any of it means

but I know that my love created you
because I was there at the moment
that you slipped screaming into this world

Angelo at 17

As we walk down Sandy Blvd
toward the Hollywood Theatre
for a screening of *Forced to Fight*

my son announces
that life has no meaning
except that which we create

He only shares such thoughts
when we walk side-by-side

his revelation providing assurance
        that whatever happens
he is going to be just fine

Keeping Score Encourages Madness

memory loop sparks contemplation
of the complexity
of my sense of responsibility
as toddler prophecy sears the heart
      like memory foam

only to dissolve into
the silhouette of a man who
      crams himself
      between two bookshelves
before the fire: feet up, cup of coffee
      set on the chess board
ancient fatigue in his eyes

The Gravity of the Situation

can't imagine ever
quite giving up on
the hope of immortality
inseparable from
the creative impulse
nevertheless
the changes in the body
are not to be denied

these days each tinge of discomfort
provokes a wave of terror
followed by a question:
Is this it—has she caught up with me at last?

> *you think you know*
> *when it's coming*
> *or you're certain*
> *now's when it ain't*

> *but you'll find that you're wrong*
> *no matter how strong*
> *your feelings may seem*

no way to know how much we're given
no way to predict when we'll be taken
only certainty: it's finite

> *don't forget*

> *don't waste it*

for the story is never finished
until the last—

[. . .]

return
now and again
and then
to the spot
wherefrom yr youthful
ejaculations sprung

the kid never died
instead had his wide-eyed vision
spread gloriously
forced open
repeatedly
for a decade or three

a tiring
but not completely defeating
torture that is
boringly
hopelessly
human

the rage
the indignation
the wonder remains

even as the foundation
of his temple
cracks and splinters
even as the gravity of loss and failure
causes the bags beneath his eyes
to pull him toward the earth
to reclaim him

Hearth and Home

by Angelo Luna

September 7, 2018
[Christopher's Birthday]

How does it feel to be a father? The same, I imagine, as it does to be a son, but in a different way. The pride of watching another being grow and change throughout the rest of our lives. It seems as if the paradoxical mindfuck of whether or not to have a child solves itself as soon as the child is born, intentional or not. Nobody knows who the best fathers in history were, but it's not a question for the ages, or even one worth asking, just look at the initials CL and choose the best course of action to take as you move towards being more like that. The sad truth of the matter is that one will die first, but it is impossible to tell which. The happy truth is that both are connected in full, heart and soul, until whatever ends they meet. Knowledge is a living fan base of all the bullshit this world produces, so get rid of all the knowledge and focus on the love. That's the real stuff, the pure stuff. Being this close in similar states of being with infinitely different lives is comparable to piloting a ship that isn't your own— you gain your footing after learning from the best before you, and then chart a new, unique course that someone has taken before, but nobody has seen. Behind the books and the beard stands a mountain of movie trivia and glorious emotion. Not to be trifled with, because there is no fighting in that beautiful landscape, only the hum of the birds, the scratch of a pen on paper, and markings of a life well lived, that is not close to over. "The world needs more of this," they both say, standing in the grass, pointing out to a majestic sunset.

Son in Silver Emerges from the Ether

How will I recognize you
the next time you approach me on the street?
After all, both of us will have
lost & regenerated
98% of our cells by then.
Will you be red, silver, or godhead?
Only The Seer Knows

Quantum Physics Equals Father and Son Eternally Swapping Roles as Student or Teacher

one day you're gonna
    have to show me
    how to do that—
how to love everyone

remind me how
    to believe
in the basic goodness
    of all beings

how to believe
    that everything
is going to be
    just fine

how to believe
    in myself
and face each day
    with a knowing smile

safe in the knowledge
    of my potential

content with things
    as they are

and motivated
    to continue
    forward

certain that
    love is all
    & all is love

Celebrate Like You're Running Out of Time
A Birthday Poem for Greg Luna

Dedicated also to Angelo Luna,
Toni Lumbrazo Luna, & Lin-Manuel Miranda

1.

separated from his love
Angelo studies stoicism
obsesses over stats
keeping an eye on the latest
from the WHO & the CDC
to tell him where his head is at
perhaps his studies will lead him
to develop the NYC grit
his mother denied him
when she tore us from our home state
so that she could spend her days hiding
all I know is I admire him
I must respect his wishes
regarding our time outside the house
he's keeping us all safe
and in return I enjoy
the gift of time with him

    it's all we have in the end

2.

lockdown inevitably changes one's perspective:

I now realize that I suffer from
    self-created
    ego-driven

paranoia
                all of which are illusion
                and a colossal waste of my
                limited time on this earth

or that I spend too many moments
worrying about bullshit

being isolated
from family & friends

        (since late 2001)

has forced me to reconsider
my concept of both freedom & independence
meanwhile
the world burns
and an evil thug
has his rich knee
on the neck of
our democracy

3.

on this day when independence from monarchy
is reduced to a mindless, heartless, nutrition-free
        cartoon of patriotism

I marvel at you
my brother
an anomaly
in our contentious family:
a truly peaceful person

[. . .]

and the only one able to
broker peace
when shit goes down

wish I had an ounce of your ease
to soothe my troubled mind
it is as if the spirit of our grandfather
his tranquility   the quiet power
        of his equanimity
had leapt into you
so that you might embody
        the harmony
this energy affords

                I love you for it

4.

yesterday as we watched *Hamilton*
crying & laughing & experiencing
a resurgence in our love for the republic

a hawk appeared suddenly on our back fence
& everything froze—you should have seen it

        yellow & red & ferocious   majestic

        & completely indifferent to our petty worries

we caught a brief glimpse of true freedom & realized

        how lucky we are to be alive right now

Atta

by Angelo Luna

Not a beat poet
but loves the beat, certainly
Smooth jazz
rapid rhythms
the claws that sink in
when an Invader
grabs you by the short and curlies
and tells you to
fucking
Dance

Not a a beat poet, no
but described by Ginsberg
decades before his existence nonetheless
First thought, best thought
Uninhibited
Uncontrolled
a radioactive substance in writing

Internal Radiation Therapy
words healing the country
from the inside out

While the world burns in
Trump's America
Bolsonaro's Brazil
God's Earth
he writes his truth, and fights fire
by sucking the oxygen out of the room
A man whose quantifiable praise for his ancestors
quiets crowds
when it's spoken out loud

[. . .]

No more fire

There aren't enough of him

Not quite zen
but buddhist in soul and practice
Does what's being said need to be said?
Why are you saying it?
Does it help anyone?
They may be mantras to some
but it's better thought of as a scientific method
dissect every interaction
future and past
and see which parts were necessary

Make yourself the best you can be

I write inhibited
Clinical
still coming into my own and learning from my betters

He teaches as a delimiter
not a time bomb
Not a beat poet, definitively,
but heavily influenced
and proud of it.
Surrealist
Grounded
visionary works
clutter file cabinets, real and digital.

Ginsberg watches him from another life
passing by on the street every chance he gets

without knowing it
I like to think that if reincarnation is
the way things go
that good ol' Allen
is younger than my father
Maybe he's a student
a fellow teacher
a preteen he makes a collage for.
Maybe he's me, though I doubt it
I have other elders to follow

Stoic principles prepare us for loss
and I'll spend my time in study preparing for his, most

Regardless of the sum of my works
or the product of his
I don't know what real life will do when he's gone.
A crack in an invisible wall
that only suffers when a truly great person leaves

There's only so many it can take
I often wonder if his
will be the last

He betters himself
works with his son to live longer
even though it hurts
and sometimes isn't as entertaining as others

He doesn't want to see that wall crack either
he wants to surpass legacies
become one of those elders

[. . .]

No, that's incorrect. Forgive my candidness,
but that's what
I
Want
He would be happy leaving a mark on a closed
small circle
I want to see his name in essays
50 years from now
Either way
I'll be proud.
He deserves it.

School Zone

by Angelo Luna

A long time ago, in a country not so far away, a few empirical hypocrites declared that children were property of the parents, blacks were property of the whites, and women were property of their husbands.

A not so long time ago, in a country much closer, an enlightened being was born with the knowledge that this was shite, and people deserve better. He taught his son this, along with knowledge of the human body, a love of obscene horror, and an open mindset. The modern-day hypocrites called it dereliction of duty; he called it freedom, and still does.

The son grew older, recognizing how hurtful the world can be, experiencing it ever so often and questioning his father about the experience. His father responded with "people who are mean to others probably don't have a good home life and have been bullied themselves. This is why it's more even important to be nice to them." So he did. More years passed and he found friendship everywhere, love (multiple times), and knowledge of how to be better everywhere he looked. Encouragement came from the patriarch at every book read, journey experienced, and thin line walked.

At age 16, he received a Driver's License, and set out on his own for the first time. Something stuck out to him: school zones. People speeding past, or abiding by restrictions, both surfaced as the same thought in his mind. They say they slow down because they care about the children, but if that was true, why would

[. . .]

we need the fines? Another thought came: his father cared about the children. Compassion is a crime when you live in a world where all you have been taught is how to suffer at the hands of others. This boy's father taught him how to suffer, and be kind despite it, doing something many others didn't— be selfless. He would make mistakes, so would the father, but actualization doesn't come from taking easy paths.

18 went by, then 19 and 20. Finally he sat at the cusp of a new life, one without restrictions, or childhood surroundings, and found a peaceful kind of gratitude that he was raised to appreciate the life he was given and will do the same for his children one day. The father will cry when he leaves, and no one but his wife will hear it. However, he'll be in good hands— she follows the same code. And still, despite the shifting tides of years to come, the son will never be too far away.

For Angelo on His Twenty-First Birthday

our love
my heart
my flesh
my blood
made real

an angel
born into
chaos & wonder
poised to embark upon
grand adventures
none could have imagined

my baby
my boy
my teacher
my friend

who saved me
when I was
beat down

who laughs
who sings
who contemplates
who loves so well
who sets goals
then takes action

who fills my heart with pride

a man, now

he flies

Afterword

Art Is My Religion:
Seeing Prophets of Rage with Angelo

Art is my religion. Every useful lesson or profound revelation I have benefited from was conveyed to me through poetry, music, dance, painting, or film. Of these, music is the most participatory. As an audience member, you can dance, sing along, scream, and freak out as the music moves through you and transforms you on the spot. I have been truly blessed by many transformative concert experiences over the years.

My son is the best thing in my life, the source of my deepest love and sense of pride. He is a remarkable person—a thoughtful, funny, philosophical, young man who challenges and amazes me every day.

Since he was born, I have dreamed of sharing a live concert experience with him. When he was a toddler, I took him to a few, including one of his first favorites: They Might Be Giants. The parents out there know that at a certain point the reliably goofy TMBG began making children's music, and they are great at it. Their children's songs have become so popular that when they tour they have to make clear which dates are kids' shows and which are adults only. I'm sure that Angelo does not remember the trip he made with me and his mother to Waterfront Park in Portland, OR. By the time the band took the stage, he was asleep in his stroller, and he did not wake up. Therefore, this early attempt to share live music with him doesn't really count.

I had offered to take him to shows before. There have always been bands and songs that both of us like such as Muse, the Black Keys, Talking Heads, Mika, and the White Stripes. However, he had no interest in seeing a live show. He did not even seem open to the idea. While I found this baffling and disappointing, I'm not the type of Dad to force him. When he was young, I often took him to poetry

[. . .]

readings and art shows, but once he got old enough to look after himself, I always left the decision up to him. I was aware that if I jammed poetry and art down his throat that I could become the reason he grew to hate them. Today my son has a real appreciation for the arts that might not have been possible if I had laid some kind of heavy expectation on him.

I was very excited to learn about the formation of Prophets of Rage, a band consisting of members of three of the best hip hop bands of all time: Public Enemy, Cypress Hill, and Rage Against the Machine. POR formed in response to the depressing shit show of [Donald Trump's] presidential campaign. Disappointed in both of our choices, and disgusted by the current state of affairs, POR nevertheless believes that we all have a responsibility to get involved. When I learned that POR was coming to the amphitheater in Ridgefield, WA, I had to be there. My wife Toni and dear friend Tiffany planned to buy me a ticket for my birthday.

I saw an opportunity to share this experience with my son when I learned that AWOLNATION would be touring with POR. Apparently, AN signed on to help POR drum up ticket sales by using their current popularity to persuade young people to buy tickets for a supergroup featuring members of bands whose popularity peaked in the 1990s. When I told Angelo that AWOLNATION would be there, he got very excited. Toni and Tiffany agreed, and it was settled.

Before the show we bought t-shirts, had some pizza and Dutch Bros. coffee. As we waited to go in, I told him some stories from my years of going to shows. I told him about the countless women in denim and leopard print clothing at the KISS show. Told him about the first time I was able to spot a narc, walking around tripping before a Dead show. I also recounted hanging out in the parking garage outside the venue in Albany because my Dead ticket was counterfeit, and the time I took LSD and danced for a long time to "Drums/Space" before finally opening my eyes to realize that I was the only one on the floor who was standing. No one tried to get me to sit down. They just let me do my thing.

We agreed that the opening act, WAK RAT, had a dumb name. We also shared the same opinion of their music. We enjoyed the metal trio's sound, but found their lyrics to be really dumb. The lead singer was a very good bass player, and the drummer and guitarist were reliably aggressive. The lead singer had a folksy, working class way about him which I liked. He sang like a regular guy. Unfortunately, when he tried to make political statements he was completely unintelligible. I liked WAK RAT much better during the instrumental parts of their songs. Despite all this, Angelo enjoyed the first set enough to suddenly declare that he'd like us to go to see Blue October or Dirty Heads together.

The true fulfillment of my dream occurred the moment that AWOL NATION took the stage. Immediately Angelo was on his feet—swaying, dancing, pumping his fist, clapping or else obeying every instruction. I was filled with an incredible happiness, to finally share one of my most meaningful experiences with my son. Angelo even enjoyed a seminal concertgoer's moment of joy when AWOL NATION played "Dreamers," the one song he really wanted to hear. I loved being able to facilitate my son's first transcendent musical moment.

Even though Prophets of Rage played many songs he didn't know, he was familiar with some of the Rage Against the Machine songs as well as a few of the hip hop tunes they played. While they played more RATM than anything else, I was very happy with the rest—"Fight the Power," "Bring the Noise," "She Watch Channel Zero," "Miuzi Weighs a Ton." B Real did a great job on the vocals for the Rage songs, and of course, they played all the big Cypress Hill tunes. I was also thrilled that Toni had bought us tickets that were close enough to the stage for me to see Tom Morello's fingers move across the frets and his facial expressions. The love he has for the music, and for the fans, was written all over his face. Chuck D has been doing this for a long time, but he showed no signs of tiring. His energy remained high, and his booming bass voice remains as strong as ever.

[. . .]

I have had a hard time enjoying many of the shows I've seen in the Pacific Northwest because the crowds have been so lame. No matter how great the performance, people regularly shout people down when they try to dance. This always makes me wonder why some people go to live shows at all. If you're not moved enough to stand when the musicians are present, why not stay home and sit on your ass while listening to the CD. It's lame and infuriating. Fortunately, the crowd at Prophets of Rage stayed on its feet for the entire show. Everyone danced, leapt, bounced, sand, and hollered together. I sang along to nearly every song, and nearly blew out my voice, which would not have been good since I had a reading the next night.

I had a great time dancing and singing and freaking out side by side with Angelo. I can die happy.

~ ~ ~

Note: Since this was written, Angelo and I have attended several shows together, including amazing sets by Dirty Heads and Tech N9ne. We had a particularly good time at the outdoor shows at the Cuthbert Amphitheater in Eugene, my favorite venue in the Northwest, despite (or because of) being drenched with rain. COVID-19 had a devastating effect on live music. We look forward to a time in the near future when we can safely return to enjoying live music performances.

A slightly different version of this essay appears on my blog: https://christopherluna-poetry.blogspot.com/2016/10/art-is-my-religion-seeing-prophets-of.html

Acknowledgments

I am indebted to so many who love my son and who have loved and supported both of us during my long exile in Ghost Town, USA. My wife and partner Toni Lumbrazo Luna has loved Angelo like he was her own since the day she met him, and has generously created a sanctuary in our home for the three of us.

I am grateful to Shawn and Robert Sanders for taking a chance on such a personal manuscript. It is always difficult for writers to find the distance needed to assess their own work, but it can be damn near impossible to do so with poems like these. I am honored that they saw the work contained in this book as fit for public consumption.

Several sections of the 100-page investigative poem "more than we can bear" appeared on Randy Roark's now defunct webzine *For Immediate Release*. "Angelo picks flowers for Dad and Ganesh" and "The Buddha of Independence Day" also appear in *Ghost Town Poetry: Cover to Cover Books 2004-2010*, published by Printed Matter Vancouver in 2011. "Things Get Serious in Ghost Town" appeared in *GHOST TOWN, USA*, a self-published chapbook from 2008 featuring my poems and observations of Vancouver, WA. "Ode to Cathleen Luna, the O.G.," "Celebrate Like You're Running Out of Time," and "Art is My Religion" appeared in slightly different versions on my blog: https://christopherluna-poetry.blogspot.com. "Father and Son, Facing the Same Way" appeared on the Clark College Foundation website and was also rendered as a permanent public art installation at the Vancouver Mall Transit Center to honor my contributions as Clark County's inaugural Poet Laureate. My thanks to Koryn Rolstad for creating this beautiful piece of art: http://www. krstudios.com/.

I would also like to thank everyone in the Ghost Town Poetry Open Mic community who embraced Angelo wholeheartedly and encouraged his early efforts at writing and performing poetry. We are

[. . .]

especially proud of those who attended our "all ages and uncensored" readings from toddlerhood and grew up with the series. Regardless of whether or not poetry becomes their vocation, each of these young people learned the value of the art form, and each of them received the love and good energy that we have come to expect from the audiences present at these readings.

Finally, I'd like to dedicate this book to my son Angelo, who saved me when I had nearly given up on life, and kept me happy enough to stick around until the love of my life appeared on the scene. Thank you for being a true friend. I am so proud of the man you've become, and I can't wait to see all the incredible things that you are going to do with your life.

Praise for *Exchanging Wisdom*

Christopher Luna is a true heir to the Beat and New York School traditions of candor and grandeur. This collaboration and celebration of life runs on impeccable timing and deep love. As Luna and his son Angelo exchange wisdom they also re-invent the meaning of open verse: these poems crack open the heart and spill the joy of parenthood into the world.

—Lisa Jarnot, author
Robert Duncan, the Ambassador from Venus

One day you're gonna have to…remind me how to believe in the basic goodness of all beings, Christopher Luna tells his son, Angelo, in his latest book. More than a collection of father-son poems, *Exchanging Wisdom* is a record of gratitude. Luna knows that to be a parent is to be both teacher and pupil, vulnerable and responsible. In every poem Luna's love beams: *Like Lone Wolf and Cub we traversed…and you reminded me that magic is real.…* These poems contemplate our never-ending wars, sickness, apathy, and artmaking through the lens of a deeply reverent father. For some, being a parent, being the *adult,* is synonymous with having the answers. Luna, a Buddhist poet, community-organizer, and activist, reminds us that questioning is the only way to truth. *What are you afraid to find?* he wonders. *Are these the right questions to ask?* In these mind- and heart-opening poems Luna invites us to *experience pure joy and wonder again through memory and thankfulness. Once you've opened those doors/ you need never do so again*, asserts Luna. Once father you cannot go back to your former life. Thankfully for us, Luna never did.

—Claudia F. Savage, author of *Bruising Continents*

In this triumphant call-and-response love letter between father and son, the epic journey of the heart is explored in wisdom, witness, wonder, actualization, and kindness. We accompany two speakers in a multi-generational reckoning of what it means to be human,

[. . .]

to be family, to embody and take forward *a love which will outlive us all*. I wept at the depth of connection I traveled in this lifesaving, life-affirming journey. As father and son are *eternally swapping roles as student or teacher*, together they inherit themselves. Angelo (the son) reflects in a poem to Christopher (his father) on his birthday, *...focus on the love. That's the real stuff the pure stuff... The world needs more of this...* This collection gives it to us real and pure. Our world is so much better for it.

—Sage Cohen, author of *Fierce on the Page*

Christopher Luna always writes with his heart on a swivel, keeping watch for moments of significance, either now or some distance from now. But *Exchanging Wisdom* is more than just a love letter to parenthood or salvation or even to his son. In the right light, this book is a star map to guide the traveler. Drink it all in. Use both hands if you have to.

—Tommy Gaffney, author
Three Beers from Oblivion and *Whiskey Days*

About the Authors

Christopher Luna is a poet, editor, teacher, writing coach and collage artist. He served as the inaugural Poet Laureate of Clark County from 2013-2017. Luna has an MFA from the Jack Kerouac School of Disembodied Poetics, and is the co-founder, with Toni Lumbrazo Luna, of Printed Matter Vancouver, an editing service and small press for Northwest writers. He founded the popular LGBTQ+ friendly, all ages and uncensored Ghost Town Poetry Open Mic in Vancouver, WA, in 2004. Christopher Luna's books include Message from the *Vessel in a Dream* (Flowstone Press, 2018), *Brutal Glints of Moonlight*, and *The Flame Is Ours: The Letters of Stan Brakhage and Michael McClure 1961-1978*.

Christopher believes that the parent-child power dynamic is inherently fascist, so he endeavored to raise his son to think for himself, question authority, and make his own decisions. He respected his son's humanity enough to trust him to be responsible, to "allow" him his autonomy. Despite what some saw as tragic indulgence, Angelo grew up to be a sweet, kind, polite, philosophical, compassionate young man who will surely accomplish things his father could not. Christopher could not imagine being more proud of the person Angelo became.

~ ~ ~

Angelo Luna is a poet, son, and LEGO connoisseur. Originally from New York, with a migration to Washington as a young child, he grew up with a fiery bloodline and cold weather. Currently employed as a teller for Wells Fargo, he loves writing, working, and finance and is interested in what every human has to offer.

About The Poetry Box

The Poetry Box® is a boutique publishing company in Portland, Oregon, which provides a platform for both established and emerging poets to share their words with the world through beautiful printed books and chapbooks.

Feel free to visit the online bookstore (thePoetryBox.com), where you'll find more titles including:

Excoriation by Rebecca Smolen

Dear John— by Laura LeHew

World Gone Zoom by David Belmont

The Catalog of Small Contentments by Carolyn Martin

Gaslight Opera by Gary Percecepe

A Shape of Sky by Cathy Cain

A Long, Wide Stretch of Calm by Melanie Green

What She Was Wearing by Shawn Aveningo Sanders

Sylvan Grove by Barbara A. Meier

Stronger Than the Current by Mark Thalman

Sophia & Mister Walter Whitman by Penelope Scambly Schott

Sitting in Powell's Watching Burnside Dissolve in Rain by Doug Stone

and more . . .